THE WHITE DEATH

Daniel Therriault

BROADWAY PLAY PUBLISHING INC
New York
www.broadwayplaypub.com
info@broadwayplaypub.com

THE WHITE DEATH
© Copyright 1989 Daniel Therriault

Cover art by Stephen Mellor

First published by B P P I in *Anti-Naturalism* in September 1989
This edition: December 2018

I S B N: 978-0-88145-819-0

Book design: Marie Donovan
Page make-up: Adobe InDesign
Typeface: Palatino

To Bill and Lowry

THE WHITE DEATH premiered at Kumu Kahua (Dennis Carroll, Executive Director) in Honolulu on 23 January 1986. The cast and creative contributors were:

KITTY KALUA ....Lei Kaniaupio
KANAKA .... James Grant Benton
KIMO.. Dave Lancaster
REV HUNTER.. Allen Cole
THE CARDINAL CODE.............................. Walt Robertson
TOURIST ....Frank B Shaner
LIONEL HARDING .... Christopher Ivanyi
OMURO .... Dennis Chun

Director...Dando Kluever
Scenery & lighting design ....Stephen Clear
Costumes..Loletia Williams
Production stage manager .... Christopher Ivanyi

THE WHITE DEATH opened in Los Angeles at the CAST Theatre through Appian Way Productions and Ted Schmitt for the CAST Theatre on 23 November 1987. It was produced by Lisa James, Linda Bernstein, and Cheryl Bascom. The cast and creative contributors were:

KITTY KALUA .... Shuko Akune
KANAKA .... Henry K Bal
KIMO .... Alberto Isaac
REV HUNTER .... Gregg Henry
THE CARDINAL CODE/TOURIST .... Royce D Applegate
OMURO .... Rob Narita

Note: There was no actor for LIONEL HARDING *in the L A production, they used a dummy.*

Director .... Charles G Davis
Set design .... Kevin Adams
Costumes .... Martha Ferrara
Lights .... Brian Gale
Sound .... Stephen Shaffer
Production stage manager .... Shawn LaVallee

CHARACTERS

KITTY KALUA, *female, Hawaiian*
KANAKA, *male, Hawaiian*
KIMO, *male, Filipino-American*
REV HUNTER, *male, white*
THE CARDINAL CODE, *male, in his sixties, white*
TOURIST, *male, in his fifties, white*
LIONEL HARDING, *male, white*
OMURO, *male, Japanese*

The role of THE CARDINAL CODE *is a voice over the telephone.*

If necessary, one actor can play the roles of THE CARDINAL CODE, TOURIST, *and* LIONEL HARDING.

The entire action erupts in the Volcano Bar, built on the rim of Kilauea Crater in the village of Volcano on the island of Hawaii. The action takes place within twenty-four hours.

The time is the present.

GLOSSARY

Pronunciation of Hawaiian

Vowels:	Rising Diphthongs:
a like a in above	ae like y in my
e like y in city	ai like y in my
i like y in city	au like ow in how
o like o in sole	ao like ow in how
u like oo in moon	oi like oi in oil

Exception: The first e in Pele and in hele is like e in bet.

' (in word itself) A glottal stop, similar to the sound between the ohs in English oh-oh. ' (in pronunciation key) A syllable accent.

HAWAIIAN

aloha (a-lo'-ha) Love, hello, goodbye.
Halemaumau (Ha'-le-mau'-mau) A volcanic crater.
haole (how'-ly). White person. Caucasian. Foreigner.
hapu'u (ha-poo') A tree fern.
hele (he'-ly) To go, come, move.
Hilo (hi'-lo) The largest town on the island of Hawaii.
hukilau (hu'-ki-lau) To fish with a seine. A fish feast.
hula (hu'-la) Hawaiian dance.
ka The.
kalua (ka-lu'-a) 1. To bake in a ground oven, baked. 2. Pit.
kanaka (ka-na'-ka) Human being, man, Hawaiian,

mankind.
kane (ka'-nay) Male, man, husband.
kapu (ka-pu) Forbidden.
Kilauea (Ki'-lau-ay'-a) Volcanic crater ruled by Pele.
koa (ko'-a) Indigenous tree and wood from that tree.
kukae (ku-kae) Feces.
lei (lay'-i) Necklace of flowers, leaves, shells, feathers.
lolo (lo-lo) 1. Crazy. 2. Stupid.
lua (lu'-a) 1. Toilet. 2. Hole that has a bottom, pit.
luau (lu'-au) Hawaiian feast.
mahalo (ma-ha'-lo) Thank you.
mahu (ma'-hu) Homosexual.
maile (mai'-le) A shrub with fragrant leaves used for leis.
makua 'uhane (ma-ku'-a u-ha'-ne) Catholic priest.
mauka (mau'-ka) Inland.
Mauna Loa (mau'-na lo'-a) Long mountain. Volcanic mountain that contains Kilauea Crater.
'ohana (o-ha'-na) Family.
okole (o-ko'-le) Buttocks.
ono (o'-no) Good, delicious.
pau (pow) Finished, done, ended.
Pele (Pe'-ly) The volcano goddess.
pilau (pi-lau') Stink, stench, bad smell, rot, decomposed.
po'i 'uhane (po'-i u-ha'ne) Soul snatching, to capture souls.
pua'a (pu-a'-a) Pig, hog, swine.
puka (pu'-ka) 1. Hole (perforation), puncture; opening.
Puna (pu'-na) Region on the island of Hawaii.
pupule (pu-pu'-le) Crazy, insane.
wahine (wa-hi'-ne) Woman, lady, wife.
wikiwiki (wi'-ki-wi'-ki) Quick, fast.

SLANG

brah (bra) Brother. Term of affection, like man or amigo.

Buddaheads (Bud'-dha-heads) Derogatory term for Japanese people.

bugger (bug'-ger) Man, guy, thing.

chee (gee) An expression of awe, confusion.

da kine (da kine) The kind, the thing, the type meant.

eeha (ee'-ha) An expression of rejoicing.

eh (ay) Hey.

Flip A derogatory term for Filipino.

garans (gar'-ans) Guaranteed.

Kanak (ka-nak') Short for Kanaka.

lava-lava A tight, wrap-around skirt, usually a floral design.

makee (ma'-kay) A Japanese word meaning dead.

manong (ma-nong') A derogatory term for Filipino.

max Maximum, limit.

Pake (Pa-kay') Chinese.

poi dog (oi as in oil) Mutt, mixed breed, not pedigree.

Portigi (paw'-ti-gee') Derogatory term for Portugese people.

shaka (sha'-ka) Good, great, all right, everything is cool.

sharkbait 1. White people. 2. Johns, customers.

wen Went.

Yakuza (Ya'-ku-za) Japanese organized crime gang.

(The Volcano Bar is a dive. Plastic leis hang on hooks, Hawaiian dolls in grass skirts wiggle, and giant artificial palm leaves loll from the ceiling with cardboard coconuts and outsized pineapples. Bottles of liquor, set in racks to protect against earthquakes, stand behind the bar itself. Barstools and a few tables with chairs inhabit the place. There is at least one window. A single door is the only public entrance. Directly opposite this entrance, another door, with the sign "Private" above it, leads to the backroom. The tavern is dirty; its walls are cracked, colors faded, and darkness rims the room.)

(KIMO is Filipino-American, small and wiry, with a fool's grin that often bursts into nervous laughter. His eyes constantly change from harmless innocence to an idiot's terror. He moves quickly about the bar and calls out in a thin, impotent voice.)

(KANAKA is full-blooded Hawaiian. On first impression, he appears to be ignorance in motion. His laugh is grotesque and he submits to an uncontrollable habit of scratching all parts of his body because he is physically diseased. He dresses in heavy work boots, long pants, and a tee shirt.)

(KITTY KALUA is a fiery, part-blooded Hawaiian. Tousled black hair falls past her shoulders and her green eyes sparkle like polished olivine. Make-up and Japanese-Hawaiian clothes highlight her best features with a sexual slant.)

(REV HUNTER is white and sits at the far table with a drink in his hand. His face is completely blocked from the audience and he remains on the outer circle of the action. KANAKA

holds KITTY's *wrist as she struggles to get free. He controls her easily, touching her as much as possible.)*

(Refer to GLOSSARY for Hawaiian pronunciation guide and dictionary of terms used.)

KITTY: Pele gon erupt this volcano! She gon explode 'cause of you, Kanak! Let me go! Pele gonna blow Kilauea 'cause of what you trying for do to me! No force me!

KANAKA: Pele no can erupt nothing.

KIMO: Please, Kanak, stop!

KITTY: Pele gon erupt this whole crater 'cause of what you doing!

KANAKA: The crater gonna blow, eh, but not because of some make-believe goddess named Pele.

KIMO: Let her go!

KITTY: The crater is saying no do this to me!

KANAKA: I gotta do it!

KITTY: Not to me!

KIMO: No force her!

KANAKA: I no scared of the mountain. Let the mountain do what it gotta do and let me do what I gotta do.

KIMO: Let her go now!

KITTY: It's against the rule.

KIMO: Against the rule!

KITTY: How many times already.

KIMO: You break the rule!

KITTY: And you know it.

KIMO: The rule!

KANAKA: The rule says I get her for free!

KITTY: You lie!

KIMO: Please, brah.

KANAKA: Nobody can stop the crater from shooting out lava. And nobody can stop me. I gotta blow, too.

KITTY: Me and Omuro made the deal. Everybody but you, brah. That's the rule. You the only one.

KIMO: You the only one!

KITTY: You know how come? Me and Omuro figure it out. You one pig. Pua'a. *(Beat)* And I no do pigs.

(KANAKA wraps one arm around KITTY'S neck. He presses himself against her; his mouth is close to her face.)

KANAKA: I'll break your neck.

KITTY: Pigs no can break necks. They just eat and lie in the mud. Get your infested body off me.

KANAKA: I'll crush your ribs, then.

KITTY: Wild boars jus' squeal and run away. Go oink and hide in the hapu'u. Get out of my face. You stink. Your breath pilau. *(Vehemently)* Never, Kanak. Never with you.

KANAKA: My ancestors royalty.

KITTY: Then you one Prince of the Pigs.

KIMO: I get customer. For my sake, Kanak. Easy, brah. *(To REV)* Having fun, sir? *(Beat)* Sit back and relax. *(Whispering)* Sorry about this guy. This never wen happen before. *(Beat)* But everything okey-dokey. Drink up and enjoy the local color.

(REV's hand, holding a drink, rises and disappears into the darkness.)

KANAKA: Okay. We sit down like nice people. Good, eh? We nice people.

(KANAKA and KITTY sit.)

KIMO: See, Kitty? He no touch you. I wen make him stop, yeah?

KANAKA: We talk business. Straight and simple. *(He takes out a small envelope from his pocket and slides it toward her.)* I get something you like. I can get more. Plenty more.

KITTY: I get one avalanche of cocaine. For me, every night she snow. Come back spring thaw. *(She pushes the packet away.)*

KANAKA: I pay then. Here! *(He slaps money onto the table.)*

KITTY: I no like your filthy money.

KANAKA: What—more? *(He slams down more money.)* Eh, I pay three time more than any tourist! Four time! *(He slams down more money.)*

KITTY: Your money more stink than you.

(KANAKA runs his hand down KITTY'S arm. She pulls away from him.)

KITTY: No touch me.

KIMO: No touch her, Kanak. Everything but touch her.

KANAKA: Shut up.

KIMO: You can do anything. As long as you no touch her. Kapu for touch her.

(KANAKA rubs the back of his hand along her jawline. She hits his hand away.)

KITTY: Leave me alone.

KANAKA: You gotta do it with me. You know why? 'Cause me, I one Yakuza. And you the Yakuza whore.

(KITTY slaps KANAKA in the face. He smiles and rubs his cheek.)

KITTY: Don't you ever call me that again. Never. You hear? I ain't no whore. *(Pause)* I one prostitute. *(Beat)* Professional. This my body. My body my business and I the ace executive. President of the corporation. I call the shots. Hold the meetings. Run the machine. I decide what for sell and when, who for advertise to and what stocks for exchange. Eh, no get confused. I use who I like. Nobody uses me. Get that through your fat skull. Nothing but business. I take the dollar, no give a cent, and no feel a nickel's worth. You understan'? *(Beat)* I'm one prossy. I no feel nothing. I run this body my way and this corporation does great.

KIMO: Kanak, what's the matter with you, eh? You never with her before. How come now?

KANAKA: Eh, Kimo, where the cash you owe us?

KIMO: First of the month tomorrow.

KANAKA: Oh, yeah? Well, it's three minutes after midnight. This the first of the month. Tomorrow is today.

KIMO: That no make sense. Please, not now. I get customer.

KANAKA: Then nail your lips shut. Runts that owe money get no right for talk.

KIMO: Please, brah. Shhh—

KANAKA: Keep your nose outta this. Go wash some glasses.

KIMO: *(Washing glasses; to REV)* Having good time, sir? You like something, jus' scream. Pretend this guy not here and enjoy. Okay?

KITTY: You hog.

KANAKA: Get in the backroom.

KITTY: Eh, I gon tell Omuro. You break the rule and you out, brah.

KIMO: Leave the bar, now.

KANAKA: I said shut up. I make you leave.

KITTY: Kimo say for get out. Jus' do what he say. You ugly pig.

KANAKA: Get in the room.

(KANAKA *shoves* KITTY *toward the backroom.*)

KITTY: No! One customer can come for me any second.

KANAKA: (*Shoving her again*) You get one customer already. Me, I your customer. (*He scratches himself.*)

KITTY: One real customer. One with no diseases. Look at you. You get every skin sickness you can think of. You get eczema and psoriasis. Rashes, warts, fever blisters. Who knows what else.

KANAKA: I don't get no V D.

KITTY: You one typhoon of germs. One infected human being. I just think of you touching me and I get sick. If we make business, I for sure puke. No joke. That's how come we made the rule!

(KANAKA *smacks her in the face.*)

KITTY: Eh, if you gonna hit me, no hit me in the face.

KIMO: Pau already!

(KANAKA *hits her in the face again.*)

KITTY: I told you, hit me any place you like. But not in the face. I get bruise. Bad for business.

KANAKA: Men that rent your face no care about bruises.

KITTY: Jus' no hit my face!

KANAKA: But if one bruise gon make you break—

(KANAKA *clamps a hand on* KITTY. *His other arm cocks back a steel fist.*)

KITTY: Not my face!

(REV *emerges from the darkness. His face is visible for the first time. He dresses entirely in black. Even his fedora is jet. The white square of his Roman collar stands out boldly and reveals that he is a priest.*)

REV: Didn't your mother ever tell you not to hit girls?

KANAKA: Sit down before I knock you down.

REV: For the love of Christ, let the woman go.

KANAKA: If I like see one comedian I go to Honolulu. (*Seeing the collar*) Eh, what we get here? Ah! Makua 'uhane, Kitty. Look. One operative in this joint. Think of that. In this dump. What a joke. More better you run home to your rectory, Padre, I hear your mother superior calling.

REV: Release her.

KANAKA: Get me mad, I step on your face. The C C never do nothing about nothing. Go play with your `feminary' friends, Father. In your little parish. Your cave. This real life. Nothing for do with you. Say Mass and pray for sinners. Pray for me. Yeah. Offer up your whole life for me. Just leave me alone.

REV: Let the lady go.

KANAKA: This not one wahine. This one mouth. And one—

REV: I know what she does and I know what you are. A hog in human clothing. Let her go. Pigface.

KANAKA: I gonna turn your other cheek.

(KANAKA *swings.* REV *ducks the punch, pulls out a .45-caliber revolver from a shoulder holster and knocks* KANAKA's *feet from under him, slamming him to his knees.* REV's *one hand grips* KANAKA's *hair while the other presses the gun to* KANAKA's *temple.*)

REV: You're right. I do pray for pigs like you. I pray
that God gives me the control not to murder you
goons. I want to blast your brains all over this bar.
Think about it. In two seconds you may never think
again.

KANAKA: Ahh!

REV: How's this steel feel? One twitch of my finger and
you're shaking hands with the devil.

KANAKA: What?

REV: I want to go all over the world and kill pigs like
you. That would make so many people happy. Got
that, pal?

KANAKA: Who are you?

REV: Cut out your tongue. Pop your ears. Break your
snout. Chop your hands. Blind the eyes of your breed.
Clear enough, muscle-brain?

KANAKA: Yes, Father.

REV: I want to kill you so bad. I can feel it. The trigger's
almost pulled. I'm gonna desecrate your temples.

KANAKA: No kill me!

REV: I'm gonna blast you. Shoot you. Kill you.

KANAKA: Have mercy!

(REV *tears his eyes from* KANAKA *and looks searchingly to
heaven.*)

REV: My God. I implore you. Let this temptation pass.

KANAKA: Let it pass! Let it pass!

(REV *becomes calm.*)

REV: Thank you, Father, for your army of angels to
battle against the Satan within.

KANAKA: Thank you, Father. Thank you.

REV: *(With ironic command)* I save souls, mister. That's my business. If I'd `a' rubbed you out, you would have been cast into everlasting damnation. That's against my conscience. I rescue souls. My curse, your luck. So I'm going to baptize you. *(Beat)* I can kill you then.

KANAKA: What?

REV: I'll be doing you a favor.

KANAKA: Huh?

REV: Once you're dead and baptized, you'll go to the big sty in the sky.

KANAKA: No!

REV: Straight to hog heaven. Do you reject Satan? *(He jerks back KANAKA's head.)* Say I do.

KANAKA: I do.

(KANAKA's head falls forward. REV delivers the following sequence extremely fast. He jerks KANAKA's head back just before each "I do".)

REV: And all his works?

KANAKA: I do.

REV: And all his empty promises?

KANAKA: I do.

REV: Do you believe in God, the Father almighty, creator of heaven and Earth?

KANAKA: I do.

REV: Do you believe in Jesus Christ, his only son, our Lord, who was born of the Virgin Mary, was crucified, died and was buried, rose from the dead, and is now seated at the right hand of the Father?

KANAKA: I do.

REV: Do you believe in the Holy Spirit, the holy C C, the communion of saints, the forgiveness of sins, the resurrection of the body, and life everlasting?

KANAKA: I do.

REV: This is the faith of the C C. This is what the C C organization believes. I give you the Christian name of Aloysius. Pigface for short. Do you acknowledge this name?

KANAKA: I do.

REV: Blink and I'll blow you to hell in self-defense. *(Pouring liquor onto* KANAKA's *head)* I baptize you in the name of the Father, and of the Son, and of the Holy Spirit. You are now born free from sin. A new creation. Alleluia, alleluia. Your brown soul is now white. Stay white. Don't become a white death. *(He blesses* KANAKA, *using his revolver to make the sign of the cross, during the following Latin.)* In nomine Patris, et Filii, et Spiritus Sancti. Amen. You're a member of the C C.

(He aims his revolver at KANAKA *and begins to squeeze the trigger.* KITTY *and* KIMO *let out a scream.)*

REV: Na. Heaven's too good for you. You deserve a tougher sentence. I give you life. *(He lowers his gun.)* Now scram. Before I shove you on a spit and barbecue.

KANAKA: Yes, Father. *(Tripping over his feet and moaning like a wounded animal, he exits through the front door.)*

KIMO: That was something. That was really something.

REV: Just another conversion.

KIMO: I never seen anybody handle Kanak like that. In fac', I never see anybody handle anybody like that.

REV: With God on your side, miracles happen.

KIMO: Not like that. Chee.

REV: *(Sliding his revolver into its holster)* Saving souls is tough nowadays. Sometimes you have to resort to brute force. *(To KITTY)* Join you?

KIMO: Join her! Sit down. Relax.

REV: *(To KITTY)* Can I buy you a drink?

KIMO: Drinks on the House!

REV: *(To KITTY)* Mind if I sit with you for the free drink?

KITTY: *(Clearly not enthralled)* Whatevers.

(REV sits at her table.)

KIMO: Alright! One Jack Daniels on the rocks. Two shots worth. Boy that Tennessee whiskey best!

REV: Easy on the ice this time. And no stir. I don't like my booze bruised.

KIMO: Okey-dokey!

REV: *(To KITTY)* I don't like anything bruised. Especially people.

KIMO: Shame on you, Kitty! How come you no say mahalo to the Father? Thank him for step in. *(He makes the drinks.)*

REV: You don't have to say anything.

KITTY: That's right. I never gotta say nothing. What I gotta thank you for anyway? That's no big deal. Eh, you like see some roughhouse, stick around here one Saturday night. We no need nobody for step in for us. Me and Kimo can handle anything. He's my protector.

REV: Heck of a job.

KIMO: Kitty, he save you.

KITTY: Save me how? Everything gonna be more bad when Kanak come back and this collar no stay.

KIMO: Now, Kitty.

KITTY: People like you always sticking their noses into other people's business. Think they can help, when they no even understan' what's going on. Always judge and try fix. Make their mark someplace they no belong, on people they don't even know. Try make you think like them. Act like them. Come off like they do you one favor. Stand up for the little lady. Pull out their gun and their conscience. Eh, I no need it. Believe me, brah. We can handle him. *(Beat)* Anyway, Kanak one nice guy when you get to know him.

REV: But I wasn't saving you. I was saving him. I save people from themselves. It's not my job to save a person from another person. That's police work.

KITTY: *(Taken off guard)* Well, good you no step in for my sake. Get me mad everytime, people try save me.

REV: I wasn't even thinking of you and for that I'm sorry. Accept my apology?

KITTY: What you trying for be? One knight in shining collar? Never mind.

REV: Thank you.

KITTY: Jus' keep your conscience in your holster, that's where it belongs.

KIMO: *(Carrying a tray of drinks to the table)* Eeha! Everybody make up! Everybody happy! Champagne for the lady. Jack Daniels—light ice, no stir—for the operative. Rum and pineapple juice for me. I like make one toast. To this operative that come to us outta the darkness.

(They drink. He makes a grand gesture.)

KIMO: Aloha. This the Volcano Bar. *(He bows.)* My name Kimo. That's Hawaiian for James.

KITTY: James English for Kimo.

KIMO: You can call me Jimmy. It's more easy for the visitors.

REV: Glad to meet you, Kimo.

KIMO: I the owner of this bar. I Filipino descent but I not member of the C C. My family somehow slip through the crack, yeah. *(He laughs, then is suddenly terrified.)* But you no try baptize me, now, Father! Please!

KITTY: No be stupid, Kimo.

KIMO: And this Kitty Kalua.

REV: My pleasure.

KITTY: I'm sure.

(Beat)

REV: What's kalua mean in Hawaiian?

KITTY: To cook underneath. But one word in Hawaiian can mean many things. Ka lua means the toilet. And I sure take a lot of kukae.

KIMO: How come you no act nice? So please, Father, what's your name?

REV: Hunter. Rev Hunter.

KIMO: Rev for reverend.

KITTY: Or revolver?

REV: Revolution. The number of revolutions per minute.

KIMO: Like rev-up!

KITTY: We never get one operative in this joint before.

KIMO: Never! *(Beat)* So where you staying?

REV: Halemaumau Hotel.

KIMO: Oh, right down the road. Eh, maybe you get lucky, gon see the eruption. Kilauea getting ready for blow. The scientists say that the pressure stay up, you know. This bar, eh, Father, she built right on the edge of the crater. In fac', half this building stay on stilts, hanging right off from the rim, into the crater. So real volcano bar, you know. You can see the whole crater right through this window over here.

(KIMO *indicates an invisible picture window that lies between the actors and the audience. When the characters look through this window, they look out onto the audience.*)

KIMO: But it kinda dark, now. You no can see nothing. You ever see the crater before?

REV: No.

KIMO: The dark hide what you no can imagine. Tomorrow bring light.

KITTY: Pele gonna blow in revenge.

KIMO: That's one treat for see the eruption! Unreal.

KITTY: She not take trash from nobody.

KIMO: Your heart bust outta your chest. You get this feeling in your guts. You always remember your first eruption. Kinda like sex. You lucky man you see that, eh, Father.

KITTY: She jus' shoot out when somebody go mess with her.

REV: What's she talking about?

KIMO: Blood Hawaiians, you know, they believe that Kilauea crater stay ruled by Pele. That she makes all the eruptions.

KITTY: She da kine woman. She wen make this crater. (*Pointing out the picture window*) Right outside this bar she made Kilauea for her fiancé. But then she saw him and her own sister making sex on the rim. She wen explode with lava and the eruption wen kill them both. Now, everytime Kilauea blows, it's Pele against something.

REV: I used to like ghost stories, too.

KITTY: Eh, no way. Pele real.

REV: My God forgives all sinners.

KITTY: Some things jus' no can be forgiven. Watch it, makua 'uhane! Pele gonna erupt 'cause you make your home on her volcano, stink up the air with that Latin and dirty her altar with baptizing Kanak!

REV: *(Deadpan)* I'm trembling.

KIMO: Please, Kitty. The operative stay our guest. Be nice. He saved you.

KITTY: He saved Kanak!

KIMO: Alright. *(Whispering to* KITTY*)* Be happy. *(Loudly)* I get more drinks. One more round on the House. *(To* REV*)* She get crazy with this Pele stuff. Gibber jabber all the time. Pele this, Pele that. This Kitty turn into one mynah bird. Pay no attention, Father. But you come back here daytime and I'll show you the crater. Magnificent view from my window. *(Emphatically)* The best view on the island! You see the sulphur shooting from the lava vents. Look like the steam trying for blow the lid off the crater. Like one rice cooker. *(He laughs.)* You see tomorrow.

REV: Is that what I smell, sulphur?

KIMO: Sulphur.

REV: Whole area reeks of it.

KIMO: More drinks coming up! *(Whispering to* KITTY*)* Cheer up.

(KIMO makes the drinks. REV places a photograph on the table.)

REV: You know this guy?

KITTY: Never seen him before in my life.

(REV *shows the photograph to* KIMO.)

REV: Ever seen him?

KIMO: President of the Hilo Sugar Company. Come in here all the time. But not for drink; for Kitty. *(Scolding* KITTY*)* What's the matter with you? How can you tell him you no know this guy? Everybody in town know you know him! *(Confidentially to* REV*)* He get killed yesterday. She one nice girl. Leave her out of it.

REV: He have a date with her yesterday?

(KIMO *nods*.)

REV: And got it right after.

KIMO: I don't know nothing.

REV: Thanks. *(To* KITTY*)* One of your customers. That's tough.

KITTY: Not. Life's one big luau.

REV: Who iced him?

KITTY: What my clients say to me stays secret, padre. You know the game. Like confession. My body's my church. They worship in it. I give them sanctuary, too. My breast the altar; my lips the gateway to paradise. You promise heaven. *(Beat)* I deliver.

REV: There ain't no heaven on earth, darlin'. And I don't care who's been ramming your sanctum.

KIMO: *(Serving the drinks)* You no can act right or what?

KITTY: How come you like for know about this guy?

REV: I'm on assignment from Rome. They can smell sin all the way to Italy on this thing. *(Beat)* I find the killer, convert him, and save his soul.

KITTY: But how come this haole death?

REV: What's haole?

KITTY: You haole.

KIMO: Haole's white.

REV: White death.

KITTY: You waste your time. The C C get no business over here. More better you work on one tan.

REV: I hate the sun.

KITTY: I love it. You wen convert our Queen. Then the soldiers came and took our islands for the U S. With guns. When you kill one people's god, you kill the whole culture. First the church, then the soldiers. That's how it always works.

REV: If I wanted a sob story, I'd go to an orphanage. *(Crossing to the telephone booth)* Besides, that wasn't us. That was the Protestants.

KIMO: You can use my phone behind the bar. No charge.

REV: Private call. *(He goes into the booth and dials. It rings.)*

(The CARDINAL CODE *is a voice over the phone.)*

CODE: The Cardinal Code.

REV: *(Into the phone)* Hunter.

CODE: Where are you?

REV: In a whiskey shack over an active volcano.

CODE: You have a nose for the hot spots.

REV: I tracked down the best prossy on the island. Took a shot in the dark that this corpse knew her. Bull's-eye. He was with her just before he punched out. She's my only lead.

CODE: I wish I could yank you off that crater. Those islands mean nothing.

REV: Rome thinks they do.

CODE: Burn Rome. Hawaii could fall to the Hare Krishnas and I wouldn't blink. *(Beat)* Chicago gave us some good times, huh, Rev?

REV: I miss the darkness. The cold. The slush.

CODE: It's all still here. Get your butt out of Rome and come back to the Windy City.

REV: I'm just checking in.

CODE: All right, I won't push. Racism's always in vogue. Let's go down that alley.

REV: I'll shoot out some streetlights. See who runs.

CODE: Watch out for falling glass.

REV: Always do.

CODE: Life everlasting.

REV: Amen. *(He hangs up and goes to the bar.)* One more Jackie D, Kimo, and have one on me.

KIMO: Mahalo. But on the House! *(He serves the drinks.)*

KITTY: When the haoles took over—

REV: Oh, Jeez.

KITTY: They made us grow only sugar cane. Now companies buy foreign sugar for more cheap. Our business go bust. Sugar killing our islands. We call it the white death.

REV: The Irish got stuck with potatoes. What else is new? *(Beat)* Listen, I hate to be a killjoy, but I gotta catch up on my jet lag.

KIMO: You come back here tomorrow. I go show you the crater. We have some laughs like that.

REV: It's a date.

KITTY: How's about a date with me, Father?

REV: There're always women who fall for the collar. I never pay for it.

KITTY: I wouldn't kiss your rosary beads.

REV: And I wouldn't leave Volcano if I were you. You're the last person to feel that dead man alive. You stay put, sister. *(He throws down the rest of his drink.)* Goodnight, Kimo. Thanks for the hooch. *(He exits.)*

KIMO: That Rev Hunter's some haole bugger, yeah? He wen make Kanak beg for mercy like that.

KITTY: Slice that hog into ham.

KIMO: Make him squeal like one stuck pig.

KITTY: Okay, now. I gonna rest up before the Hotel closes. Maybe one customer make tracks over here, yeah. Knock two times if sharkbait come in. I let you get one drink outta him, then I come out ready.

KIMO: Routine.

KITTY: Shaka, brah. *(She exits into the backroom.)*

KIMO: Chee, that Rev Hunter, boy, he get some da kine, eh. Power. Wonder how it feel be like him?

(KANAKA enters with a drawn, long-bladed fishing knife.)

KANAKA: Where the operative?

KIMO: He no stay.

KANAKA: He went?

KIMO: Pau already.

KANAKA: Good, then, brah. Oooee! That haole, he do me to the max. No lie. *(He inserts the knife into a leather sheath hanging from his belt.)* How's it? Where the puka?

KIMO: C'mon, Kanak, no start up again.

KANAKA: I gonna do her.

KIMO: You no can do nothing.

KANAKA: Where she went?

KIMO: What's the matter with you?

KANAKA: *(Throbbing)* I'm a man. That's what's
the matter with me. I decided tonight I'm a man.
(Whispering) A man. *(Matter-of-factly)* Nothing for get
excited about. Simple. No big deal.

KIMO: How come you acting lolo tonight?

KANAKA: I gonna get her. That's how come.
(Emphatically) I need her. You know?

KIMO: You know you no can get her.

KANAKA: Gimme one beer!

(KIMO gets KANAKA a beer.)

KANAKA: Eh, Kimo, me, I just one regular guy, yeah.
No different. The same like whoever. Anybody you
like me to be. Everybody. Nobody. Yakuza.

KIMO: She free to all the Yakuza, but not for you, you
know why, 'cause you full of disease. She catch and
spread them.

KANAKA: Shut up about my diseases! *(Beat)* You no
can catch nothing from me. I not contagious. When
you touch me, you no become me. I keep my diseases
inside, brah. In my blood. You never can catch that.
Besides, me and Kitty both Hawaiian. She no can catch
what she already get.

KIMO: You're crazy, you know that.

KANAKA: I just common everyday kinda guy. After
work joe, eh. I get one regular need. You know, da
kine. I like slip my blade into her sheath. Simple.
No big deal. Okay? Everybody can get her. Well, so
should I. No take that away from me, too. Not that. *(In
confidence)* So Kimo, what you think, eh, you can fix me
up with her or what? Maybe I let you slide on one of
your payments, you know. Get her for do it with me. I
know I nothing special. But maybe if you pretend I'm
some Korean or tourist. Anything but me. Maybe if

you, Kimo, you go send me in there, she go do it with
me, then. You do that for me, brah?

KIMO: I ain't get nothing for do with her like that.
Anyway, Kitty no stay.

KANAKA: Where she went?

KIMO: She wen split. I dunno. So calm down.

KANAKA: I no need calm. I need Kitty.

(A TOURIST enters. He is middle-aged and costumes himself
in a gaudy aloha shirt, loud bermuda shorts, a hat, and thong
slippers. A flowered lei and a camera hang around his neck.
He's a fast talker. To him, everything exists for his pleasure.)

TOURIST: (Loudly upon entrance) Howdy!

(Recognizing the bait, KIMO snaps into a coolie act. He
dumps ashtrays, wipes the bar, nods his head, and laughs
whenever the TOURIST laughs. KIMO smiles so much that it
hurts.)

KIMO: Please, come in, sir!

TOURIST: Dang, it's colder than a cow's teat in a
blizzard. I thought this was Hawaii.

KIMO: We get you hot right away.

TOURIST: Now you're speaking my language.

KIMO: (Making a grand gesture) Aloha. This the Volcano
Bar. My name's Kimo. That's Hawaiian for James.

TOURIST: Gimme that again.

KIMO: Kimo.

TOURIST: That's hilarious! I'll never remember that.
I'll just call you Jimmy-boy. It's shorter. Well, this is
some kind of decor. (Pointing) Pineapple, right? You
people really know how to do a place up. Something
to write home about. (Confidentially and quickly) Well,
listen, Jimmy-boy, mind if I don't introduce myself?
Gotta keep things under cover. I've had my nose to the

grindstone for a full year so I'm entitled to a little fun. My wife's asleep and what she don't know won't hurt her. I hear you can give me the vacation I'm looking for.

KIMO: *(With theatrical charm)* No worry, sir. You wen enter your Polynesian Palace of Pleasure! Home of the Big Island Princess. Exotic excitement, garan ball bearin's. She come out couple minutes.

TOURIST: Hey, I ain't buyin' no warn-out mare. I'm lookin' for a filly bitin' at the bit.

KIMO: She not busy that way. She be wikiwiki.

TOURIST: Wikiwiki. You people always say things twice. That kills me. That means quick, don't it? Wikiwiki means quicky-quicky. Well, that's what I'm here for. *(He laughs.)* Get it? See, I speaky-speaky that Hawaiian stuff!

(TOURIST laughs, as does KIMO.)

TOURIST: The bartender at the Hotel said she was a real volcano, make a dead man erupt. I'll take her.

KIMO: You like, you get.

(KIMO knocks twice on the backroom door. KANAKA snaps his head toward KIMO, glares at him intensely, and then looks away.)

TOURIST: What's her name?

KIMO: Kitty.

TOURIST: Ah, a purrin' kitty-cat. I like that fine.

KIMO: What you like for drink, sir?

TOURIST: Don't want to diminish my love potential.

KIMO: One drink minimum, Tourisan.

TOURIST: One drink might just grease the pump, won't it. What's that funny drink you got here?

KIMO: Mai Tai?

TOURIST: That's the one. Like my tie. Get it? My tie.

(KIMO *and* TOURIST *both laugh.*)

TOURIST: You fellas don't wear ties, though, do you?

(*The* TOURIST *puts money on the table.* KIMO *serves the drink and takes the money. The drink is garnished with a large slice of pineapple.*)

TOURIST: Yep. You all got a beautiful little country out here. I'm thinkin' of settlin' down 'round these parts when I retire. Florida's so darn crowded. Might just park my butt on this island to die. (*Beat*) What do you think of Americans?

KIMO: I stay American.

TOURIST: I'm sure you're a citizen and everything, but I mean the folks who were born here.

KIMO: I stay born here.

TOURIST: (*Taken off guard*) In the U S of A? (*Beat*) How come you talk like that?

KIMO: I always stay talk this way.

TOURIST: Oh! You mean you were born here in Hawaii. Oh! But you're not from.... Let me ask you this then. What do you think of like Americans from Iowa? I been there and it ain't much different from Nebraska. Lotta hogs instead of cattle. I'm from Grand Island, Nebraska, myself. Born, raised, and stuck. The center cut of this great country of ours. What do you think of folks like us?

KANAKA: (*In a low, rumbling voice*) What does he think of real Americans.

TOURIST: Yeah—well no, not real—you know what I mean—hey, that's funny! (*He points at* KANAKA *and laughs.*) A real kidder. You Hawaiians are the funniest dern people, that's why me and the missus just keep on coming back!

KIMO: You mean mainlanders.

TOURIST: That's the word I'm lookin' for. Thank you, Jimmy-boy. I'm a mainlander. You're island Americans. Gee, it's funny to think of America as an island, ain't it?

KIMO: I think mainlanders are great.

TOURIST: That's all I wanted to know! You think we're great. Beautiful. *(To* KIMO*)* I can tell you're a real Hawaiian. Injun blood.

KIMO: No, I not.

TOURIST: You sure as heck look Hawaiian.

KIMO: This guy over here, Kanaka, he stay full-blood Hawaiian.

TOURIST: You're an honest-to-God native? No kidding? I gotta get a picture of this. *(He takes a picture of* KANAKA. *To* KIMO*:)* Could you snap one of the two of us together?

*(*KIMO *takes the shot.)*

TOURIST: Much gracías, amigo.

KIMO: The lady you gonna stay with, she get blood Hawaiian, too, you know. But she kinda poi dog. Mixy-mixy blood.

TOURIST: Woooeee! I'll have to get a picture of her, too, for my private collection. Know what I mean? A genuine souvenir. Gonna teach that little girl how to hula Nebraska style. *(He winnies.)* We went to a black sand beach today. I know the sign said and the tour guide said, but no one on the bus took any, so why not? I'm only one person. What the heck, I grabbed some. *(He takes out a small plastic bag full of black sand.)* Pretty stuff black sand, don't you think? Crushed lava rock. Gonna show it to the folks back home. I love this country. Even like the stores. Like those naked posters of Pele. Fine-looking goddess. Wouldn't mind dippin' into her crater. *(He sniggers. Abruptly:)* While I think of it, how would either of you boys like a job? I know all you *(Winking)* kanes are always on the rampage for some wampum, right? Well me and the missus need a driver just 'til the end of the week. All you do is take us where we want, from one hotel to another, load and offload our suitcases. Oh, I don't have to explain. You boys must do it all the time. Any takers? It's good money. If you're smart you could save enough money to vacation in Nebraska. Think about it. Bet you need a new surfboard or something. Anyhow, when I finish branding this filly, you give me your answer. Speaking of business, where is that little geisha girl?

(KITTY enters, ready to act her role. She is barefoot and dressed in a Ti leaf skirt, a Hawaiian-print bikini top, and a maile lei. Colorful sea shells encircle her ankles, wrists, waist, neck, and head.)

KIMO: *(Proclaiming)* Here she comes! Princess of the Volcano! Our own lava flow! Kitty Kalua!

KITTY: Aloha, Mac. Welcome to my mountains. I like haole boys. I like you. How you like for plunge into my volcano?

(KIMO flips a switch and recorded Tahitian drums play. The music is fast and pounding.)

TOURIST: Woooeee! Aloha my jungle kitten!

(KITTY dances Tahitian, swinging her hips back and forth with the beat of the drums. She begins teasingly and sensuously, then builds to a furious pitch. At the peak, on cue, KIMO shuts off the music.)

KITTY: I get so hot when I dance. I don't know why I wear so much clothes. I go get more comfortable. When

I'm ready *(Pointing to a light above the backroom door)* the light goes on. We talk business, then we make business for how you like.

TOURIST: Darlin', my eyes ain't gonna stray from that there bulb.

KITTY: Aloha for now. *(She exits into the backroom.)*

TOURIST: Oh my Lord, Lord, Lordy. Whatcha say her name was? Pussy?

KIMO: Kitty.

TOURIST: Same thing. In Hawaiian that's Pussy-Pussy, ain't it?

(The TOURIST howls. KANAKA looks him dead in the eyes for the first time. He has lost his hysteria; what remains is an intense focus of purpose.)

KANAKA: Take off your pants.

(Pause)

TOURIST: Sorry, buddy, I didn't catch that.

KANAKA: Take off your pants.

(Silence)

TOURIST: *(Bursting into laughter)* You people say the strangest things! You really do. Take off your pants. Oh, I gotcha. Take'em off now before I go in with the lady. Some kinda custom. Well, I been through the hukilaus. Skip the pants number. Tell you the truth, you put a scare into me a second there.

KANAKA: Haole no understand English? Take. Off. Your. Pants. *(Lifting his knife from its sheath)* Now.

(The TOURIST takes off his pants.)

KANAKA: Throw them to the bartender.

(The TOURIST does.)

KANAKA: This Kimo. Say hello Kimo.

TOURIST: Hello Kimo.

KANAKA: Kimo nice name.

TOURIST: Kimo nice name.

KANAKA: Stop the coolie act, Kimo. No tourist talk. Stay the manong you are. How much?

KIMO: Eight-hundred dollars.

KANAKA: You dumb haole.

TOURIST: I'd like to know—

KANAKA: So you like our island, yeah, cowboy?

TOURIST: Very much.

KANAKA: What you like? *(He clips the TOURIST's hat off his head with the knife.)*

TOURIST: I like everything.

KANAKA: You like the flowers? *(He cuts the lei from his neck. The flowers drop to the floor.)* You like for take pictures of the natives? *(He slices the strap and the camera falls to the floor.)* You like aloha shirts?

(KANAKA runs the blade down the TOURIST's shirt, slicing the buttons off in one smooth stroke. He takes the shirt off the TOURIST, revealing a body naked except for a pair of boxer shorts with the word ALOHA! printed across the front.)

KANAKA: You wear what you think look Hawaiian down to your underwear. You dress up like this for mock us?

TOURIST: No.

KANAKA: If not for make fun, then you like for be us.

TOURIST: I want to be like you.

KANAKA: You like the beaches? *(Offering the sand)* Eat.

TOURIST: What?

KANAKA: We get the islands deep inside. More deep than your heart. Only way you get the beaches inside you, haole. You like be Hawaiian? Eat the sand. Ono.

(The TOURIST *eats the sand. He chokes.* KANAKA *drags him behind the bar and puts a bottle to the* TOURIST's *mouth. The* TOURIST *drinks and stops coughing.)*

TOURIST: If it's money you want, take it.

KANAKA: I no like your stink money.

TOURIST: This joke has gone far enough, boys.

KANAKA: Say `boys' one more time and I cut out your tongue.

KIMO: No, Kanak, please.

(The bar conceals all action below their waists. KANAKA *cuts off the* TOURIST's *underwear and throws them in front of the bar. The light above the back room switches on red.)*

KANAKA: Without our clothes you're naked.

TOURIST: I'm sorry if I said something wrong. Maybe I stepped outta line. I got a couple of kids. I'm just a regular guy.

KANAKA: If I go to Nebraska, you let me act like you? No way, pally. Me, I regular guy jus' like you. Two things different. I get the knife. And this not your island.

*(*KANAKA *clamps a hand around the* TOURIST's *throat. The* TOURIST's *body accidently hits the switch and the Tahitian drum music comes on.)*

KANAKA: Repeat. I love your island for steal from.

TOURIST: I love your island to steal from—

KANAKA: Your goddess for make fun.

TOURIST: Your goddess make fun—

KANAKA: Your men for carry my bags.

TOURIST: Your men carry my bags—

KANAKA: Your women for do it to.

TOURIST: Do it—

(KITTY enters, wearing a kimono.)

KANAKA: How you gonna do it to our women without this?

KIMO: No!

(The hand wrapped around the TOURIST's neck disappears below the bar, followed by the swift knife. The TOURIST screams.)

KANAKA: How you gonna do anything with no life?

(KANAKA plunges the knife seven times into the TOURIST. KITTY screams. KANAKA lets the carcass fall to the floor behind the bar. He becomes drained of all energy and dazed. Pause)

KITTY: What you wen did?

KIMO: I try to stop him.

KITTY: You stupid or what?

KIMO: He never listen to me.

KITTY: How dare you butt into my business?

KIMO: How dare he kill in my bar!

KITTY: You get no right for touch my customer.

KIMO: He get no right for murder in my bar.

KITTY: You dummy!

KIMO: Blood all over!

KITTY: Stupid idiot!

KIMO: Stink in the air.

KITTY: That's my customer!

KIMO: It's my bar!

KITTY: Mongoloid!

KIMO: Blood bad for business!

KITTY: He's dead before he paid me!

(KANAKA throws the TOURIST's money into the air. KITTY picks up some bills.)

KIMO: The House rule says no murder in my bar!

KITTY: You get no right for cut my stuff.

(KANAKA switches off the music.)

KANAKA: You no even dance Hawaiian. You dance Tahitian.

KITTY: I dance for get more money from him.

KANAKA: *(Almost inaudibly)* This not his island.

(Silence)

KITTY: We gotta make one plan.

KIMO: That's what we need!

KITTY: We gotta act fast.

KIMO: I get dead tourist in my bar! *(He laughs hysterically.)*

KITTY: Stop it! *(Beat)* Burn his clothes in the rubbish can out back, then throw the ashes in the hapu'u. Scrub this bar so hard one dog no can smell one whiff of blood. But first put the body into one pineapple sack. Hele! Now!

(KIMO runs behind the bar and crouches down to the corpse, out of sight.)

KIMO: He still bleeding!

KITTY: Kanak, you go dump the body.

KIMO: What I gonna do with—his—da kine?

KITTY: Throw it in the bag with the body. Stupid!

(KIMO *runs around like a madman. He collects the*
TOURIST's *clothes and throws them into a bag, except for the*
camera. He shoves as much money as he can into his pockets
and begins to scrub the top of the bar with a sponge.)

KITTY: Eh, remember. Kanaka never came back here
tonight. *(To* KANAKA*)* I no cover up for you, pig. I
protecting Kimo. Not you, porker.

KIMO: *(Wiping the blade and* KANAKA's *hands clean)* I gon
bury the knife.

KANAKA: My knife.

(KANAKA *slides the knife into his sheath and comes out from*
behind the bar with the bag full of body. He drags the burlap
load unconsciously as if it actually were a sack of pineapples.
The sack leaves a trail of blood behind. KIMO *squats with the*
sponge and follows the bag across the room, wiping up the
path of blood and whimpering to himself.)

KITTY: Shh. Listen. *(She looks out the picture window.)*
Kimo, stop crying. Shut up!

KIMO: *(Trying to control himself)* What?

KITTY: One beautiful sound.

KIMO: I no hear nothing.

KITTY: Beautiful nothing.

KIMO: You going lolo now, too?

KITTY: No eruption.

KIMO: No Pele.

KITTY: Not. Pele's here. But she no making no noise.
She not mad for what you did, Kanak.

KIMO: Pele say Kanak good?

KITTY: She say yes. She never like the tourist either!

KANAKA: Pele get nothing for do with it. This jus' the
still before the storm.

KITTY: No matter what you say, Pele love you for killing the tourist. She thought he was one dumb haole, too. *(She laughs. Suddenly, in a silky voice:)* Kanak. Go quick. Anybody can walk in.

KIMO: *(Quietly)* Take care yourself, brah.

(KITTY approaches KANAKA impulsively. She gently touches his lower lip with one finger and rubs his lip smoothly back and forth.)

KITTY: *(Directly into his eyes)* Try stay safe.

KANAKA: Eh, Kimo, I sorry for mess up your bar. And thanks for mop-up. Kitty, I sorry for mess up your customer. And thanks for touch my lip.

(KANAKA exits with the body. KIMO continues to clean as the lights fade to a blackout, then immediately come up on KIMO setting up the bar for the new work day. It is dawn. The sun rises during this scene, though the bar remains dim since the small window is filthy. Edgy from paranoia and giddy from no sleep, KIMO is a mess. He sniffs around the bar. KITTY inhales a line of cocaine.)

KITTY: Stop sniffing all around, Kimo! Scrub, sniff. Scrub, sniff. This place one bar, all right. One bar of soap! *(Beat)* Time for quit. Get some sleep.

KIMO: The sun wen come up already. Okay. Me, I pau. Nobody gonna know what happened here last night.

KITTY: Especially that demon with the gun.

(The backroom door flies open. KANAKA bursts in. KIMO screams.)

KIMO: You scare me, Kanak! What, you lolo come busting into my bar like that?

KITTY: No come through my room! What's the matter with you? What if I get one customer? What if I by myself?

KANAKA: Forget it.

(Beat)

KITTY: You wen get rid of it?

KANAKA: Yeah. I wen did it. *(Beat)* Then I talk to Omuro. He say no problem. His goons in the police gon bury the case. Jus' another dumb tourist accident.

KITTY: With knife holes in the body?

KANAKA: I wen take care of the knife pukas. Me, I fool everybody. No worry. *(Beat)* But let me tell you about this devil in one collar! Look like we get one important bugger here. You should see Omuro's face when I wen tell him the name Rev Hunter. That yellow man turn white. *(Beat)* Hunter get big reputation. But watch it, brah. He's dangerous. Master of conversion. *(Beat)* When Hunter catch you break the law, he no tell the police. That's too easy, eh. He shuts up about your sin. Not even one judge in court can make him talk. No, what Hunter do to you more bad than the death penalty. *(Beat)* He change you. *(Beat)* He make you believe in things you no believe in. Make you act like people you no like. *(Beat)* He's one conversion machine.

KITTY: Hunter no can make me different.

KANAKA: He brainwash you so bad, brah, that you wake up years from now, look around, and you get one wife, three kids, and one boring job.

KIMO & KITTY: No!

KANAKA: Yeah! *(Beat)* Hunter wen baptize me, eh. But me, I no different. Look how I wen did the tourist.

KIMO: You not changed.

KITTY: You the same.

KANAKA: Force-baptism. That no count. *(Beat)* He's one thief. But what he steals is your soul.

KITTY: Po'i 'uhane!

KANAKA: How I wen did that tourist, Hunter can do to your soul. He stabs right through your chest, more deep than your heart and rips your soul right out from under your flesh.

(KITTY *and* KIMO *gasp in terror.*)

KANAKA: I never touch one soul. *(Beat)* The Yakuza protects you and pays you, yeah?

KIMO & KITTY: Yeah.

KANAKA: The C C kills your soul, then asks for money.

KITTY: He never get me.

KANAKA: Me neither! *(Beat)* He jus' like one shark. Sleeps with his eyes open. Always on the hunt for one more soul for eat.

(KIMO *glances out the window and shrieks.*)

KIMO: Eh, the bugger coming!

(*They all scream.*)

KANAKA: *(Having scared himself)* I gotta get outta here! *(He runs toward the backroom.)*

KITTY: No go through my room!

KANAKA: I collect tonight, Kimo! Pay you then, Kitty!

KITTY: Go out the front!

KANAKA: Eh, I not sharkbait!

(KANAKA *exits through the backroom.* REV *enters through the front door.*)

KIMO: Ah! Famous man in my bar! You one big shot.

REV: Where'd you hear that?

KIMO: Everybody know you one big wheel.

REV: I couldn't sleep. Sometimes I just can't keep my eyes closed.

(Beat)

KIMO: You hungry? Like small fish? No look at me.

KITTY: *(Whispering)* Stupid, Kimo.

REV: How about a nightcap, instead?

KIMO: On the House for the big cheese.

REV: Surprised to see your lights on. You having an early day or late night?

KIMO: I no can sleep. Business been slow. This place real murder last night. *(He mispours a drink.)* Oops! I spill. No worry. I mop up. I good for mop things up. *(He tries to subdue a laugh but fails.)*

REV: You ever been to a morgue? Never smells clean. Always the antiseptic trying to cover up the stink of death. *(Beat)* You've doused this place with ammonia.

KIMO: I do big clean-up every once in a while. *(Innocently)* How come you here?

REV: Our date, remember? There it is. *(Looking through the picture window)* Would you look at that. What all the tourists come to see. Kilauea Crater.

KIMO: Best view on the island!

REV: You mean that, don't you. Last night I had no idea this thing was so big. *(Abruptly)* Who came in here after I left?

(KIMO drops his drink.)

KIMO: Oh, boy. I so clumsy this morning. Ah. No body. No body after you. No. *(Beat)* Body. *(He cleans up the mess.)*

REV: That's funny. I was closing down the Hotel bar when in came a woman screaming that her husband was gone. Bartender said he sent the poor guy over here.

KITTY: No need cover for me, Kimo. Tourist come in, make business and split. So what?

REV: He's dead.

KITTY: What do you know.

REV: That's my question.

KITTY: Nothing.

REV: Even a corpse gets sanctuary, huh? The living are sacred, honey, not the dead. Police dogs found him at the botton of the crater. Cops were on him like lice. I couldn't get a good look at him.

KIMO: Hard for tell when the body in the bag.

(KITTY shoots him a look.)

KIMO: They throw the body in the bag real quick. Police body bag. Or was the body out of the bag? In the bag or outta the bag? Body. Bag.

REV: You need some rest, Kimo. *(Beat)* Or better, a drink. *(To KITTY)* Go dress your face. Kimo and I want to talk.

KITTY: There's no secrets with me and Kimo.

REV: Man talk.

KITTY: I bartend for you, Kimo, get some sleep.

KIMO: We go talk man to man. *(Strongly)* Go to your room.

KITTY: *(To REV)* You think you're real tough, yeah, Hunter?

REV: That makes two, darlin'. You're a regular black widow spider. A date with you and you're dead.

KITTY: Watch him, Kimo. Mahu, I think. You boys have fun. No kissing. *(She exits into the backroom.)*

KIMO: Be nice! *(Suspiciously)* How come you like talk with me?

REV: Just taking you up on the free drink.

KIMO: Celebrate you top dog!

REV: I like you by yourself.

KIMO: I good company. Me alone. You like Kimo! Whiskey, sir?

REV: Now you're talking. But don't call me sir. You say sir too much. What are you having?

KIMO: Too early I think. Well. Maybe tiny one. *(He gets the drinks.)*

REV: That a man. *(Looking around)* Must've felt great when you bought this place. Local boy makes good. To your bar.

KIMO: My bar.

(KIMO and REV drink.)

REV: Too bad you don't run it.

(Beat)

KIMO: What you mean? I stay here all the time.

REV: You serve drinks. That's all. You don't run this bar. Kanaka owned this place last night. Kitty runs the show at times. And I bet there're others.

KIMO: I the owner. What I say goes.

REV: You don't even charge for drinks. How much booze have I drunk in here for free? You're even a coolie to your customers.

KIMO: I like you. I let people I like get away with things.

REV: You're impotent.

KIMO: I not impotent!

REV: A joke in your own joint.

KIMO: It's not my fault.

REV: Of course not. You're not naturally weak inside.

KIMO: No, I not.

REV: It's bad influences.

KIMO: Bad people.

REV: Bad conditions.

KIMO: The Yakuza!

REV: Ah. That's a tough jam.

KIMO: Nobody go up against the Yakuza. They Japanese but they get some Hawaiians, now. Was more better before the Yakuza wen get Kitty. When it jus' me and her. We jus' did what we like. *(Strongly)* I not one pimp. I never get no cut. I even give her free room. And never wen sleep with her. Not one time. Me and Kitty, we stay like brother and sister. 'Ohana.

REV: Is that why she treats you like you have no—

KIMO: *(Interrupting)* Yakuza give her lotsa coke. She half outta her mind, now. We gotta do what the Yakuza like.

REV: Last night Kanaka said you owe money.

KIMO: Protection pay.

REV: From who?

KIMO: The Yakuza.

REV: Who do you pay?

KIMO: The Yakuza.

REV: You pay them to protect you from themselves?

KIMO: I not supposed to tell you this.

REV: Just think if you said to Kanaka "Leave my bar." And he answers, "Whatever you say, boss," and leaves.

KIMO: *(Laughing)* For you he go; for me, never.

REV: It could happen. But you need an organization with muscle behind you. Just like the Yakuza. No man can stand alone. He needs conglomeration. Just think.

You walk into this bar, your bar, and with one shot, clear out the whole joint.

KIMO: Never.

REV: You'd be the big shot.

KIMO: I always like get one class place. But I make one big mistake from the start. I never get no rules. This place complete chaos. Now I gotta serve criminals, prostitutes, and tourists. *(Beat)* But I still get dreams, eh. Sometimes I think like this place is one first-class restaurant. But jus' gourmet Filipino food. Spicy beef with almonds in the peanut sauce. Ooh, the best in the world. The backroom over there, that the kitchen. All good, modern appliances. I stay cooking back there. And when I become one big success, I can teach one young kid my style and how for make good like me. Then I serve my original drinks, Kimo Specials, in long-stem, crystal snifters. The whole bar look like the Philippines. Get like jungle everywhere. Lace drapes. Chandeliers. Son of a gun. The Maitre d', he in one white tuxedo. And the Filipino waitresses in brocade sarongs and transparent silk blouses. Boy. Not a lot of tables, jus' choice ones. All private. Nice, polished koa wood and each chair one tiny throne. Reservations months in advance. And somebody say something stupid I no like, I jus' tell my bouncers, eh, throw him out, jus' like that. No tourists. Jus' good people. Locals. Then I get respect. Hold my head up. Then I can be one big shot.

(Beat)

REV: You can have that.

KIMO: What?

REV: Just join the C C.

KIMO: What you talking about?

REV: You can have your restaurant.

KIMO: How?

REV: I baptize you. Then you refuse to pay the Yakuza.

KIMO: I no can do that!

REV: You can if you're a Soldier for Christ. The Yakuza is only one country. The C C is all countries. I make one phone call and a platoon of Italian Specials are here in twenty-four hours. Emergency? A planeful of Mexicans in the time it takes to untangle a scapular. These Buddha-thumping Japanese are nothing. Let us take care of you, James. Don't be afraid. Follow me.

KIMO: I will.

(REV *dips his fingers into his drink and sprinkles* KIMO's *head.)*

REV: James, I baptize you in the name of the Father, and of the Son, and of the Holy Spirit. Your brown soul is now white. Stay white. Don't let your soul become a white death. *(He takes a drink, then looks at* KIMO *calmly.)*

KIMO: That's it?

REV: That's it.

KIMO: I member of the C C?

REV: Is the Holy Spirit a bird?

(Beat)

KIMO: Me and you on the same side, now? Me and famous person! No more Yakuza. I get my restaurant. More drinks!

REV: It's not that simple. You're whitewashed. But now you've got to go further.

KIMO: Where?

REV: One complete revolution. You've got to rev up. *(Beat)* You can do it, James. You're as tough as a steel crucifix.

KIMO: Whatevers.

REV: A Soldier can't be a weak, sniveling idiot. You have to face yourself. There's something about that tourist last night.

KIMO: Please. I—

REV: This cup won't pass from you. The tourist.

KIMO: Father—no—

REV: People never tell their real sins in confession. I'm gonna tell you yours. You do whatever people expect of you. You're a sucker for the Yakuza. You butt-kiss any tourist. You don't even have the guts to be a pimp. So you're a eunuch and a free ride to a coked-up prossy. (Beat) You're not a pretty picture, James. The tourist came in. What did he do?

KIMO: He wen make me mad.

REV: That's it.

KIMO: Push my face for grin. Make my hands serve him.

REV: Deeper. Go on.

KIMO: I love the tourist. But I like for kill him. He pay me for smile. I keep him happy. I eat. Buy clothes. Stay zero. When all's pau, the tourist make me nothing. (Beat) The knife wen stab his stomach. My mouth say no, but my eyes go yeah. The tourist wen scream. Me, I happy. His blood run down. Beautiful. His screams was music. The knife push. He wen jump like one little puppet. He go dance for my tune. Jus' this one time. (Beat) But I no wen did it. I no get the guts. I'm always stay one coolie. I wen wrestle with the body, mop up the blood, cover the stink. Even when he's dead, I still serve the tourist. I love Kanak for kill the tourist. But I tell you something. I never gonna mop up for nobody again. Nobody. Never.

(The front door flies open. Blazing white light from outside shatters the darkness of the bar. A body flies mid-air through the doorway, hits the floor, and rolls to a halt. REV pulls out his revolver, spins to the window, and looks out. He moves toward the door but as soon as he hits the white light, his body freezes, caught in the brilliance. Covering his eyes, he struggles toward the opening and rolls out of sight through the doorway. KITTY enters and runs to KIMO in amazement.)

KITTY: Kimo, what, you stupid? You wen squeal on Kanak.

KIMO: I did? No, we was talking about me. Not Kanak. How you know? Stay listen at the door?

KITTY: Yeah. And you said Kanak wen did him.

KIMO: I did? He one operative. He no can say nothing. Look, another dead body in my bar! I did? Did I?

KITTY: How do all the dead haoles find this bar?

(REV enters and approaches the body, which is sprawled in an unnatural position. The corpse is white, handcuffed, barefoot, and dressed in an expensive lounging robe. The head is covered with a black hood; a shank of rope is tied around its neck.)

REV: *(Dazed from the sun)* Couldn't see a thing. Sun blinded me.

KITTY: Up the volcano the sun strong, yeah. What's the matter, operative? You no can take Pele's light? Her truth too powerful? You lose sight of your aim? Pele rob you of your vision?

KIMO: Father, a note.

KITTY: If jus' the sun blind you, wait 'til Pele blow the crater. She make you fry, haole, like one white chunk of fat.

REV: Read it.

(KIMO *takes the note from the face of the hood.*)

KIMO: `Rev Hunter: Leave these islands or you'll be the next white death.'

(REV *loosens the rope and removes the hood from the corpse.*)

KITTY: Lionel Harding.

KIMO: President of Puna Sugar.

REV: (*Giving* KIMO *a business card.*) Just in case something happens to me, here's The Cardinal Code's phone number. Trust him like sunrise. But right now, call the police. Tell them the head of Puna Sugar just dropped in. Let them know you run things around here. For the first time you'll be telling the truth. (*Slipping on a pair of sunglasses*) You're with me now, kid.

(REV *starts for the front door as the lights fade to a blackout, then immediately come up on* KITTY *and* KANAKA, *counting money. It is twilight. The sun slowly disappears during this scene. The bar becomes darker as night descends, and hotter as the volcano boils.*)

KITTY: Crater ready for blow. Pele mad at something.

KANAKA: Sun going down but it more hot. Me, I sweating like one pig.

KITTY: Smell like one, too.

KANAKA: Then give me back that stink money coming from my smelly hand. But no, you sniff Yakuza pay like it's perfume.

KITTY: If this perfume, it's cheap. This only half what my pay's supposed to be.

KANAKA: Omuro say he get cut on your personal customers.

KITTY: That not the deal we made.

KANAKA: The deal's what Omuro say the deal is.

KITTY: Not with me. I trick all Yakuza for free. But my personal clients stay mine. I think Yakuza doing it to me more ways than one.

KANAKA: What you crying for? You jus' get three-thousand dollars worth of free cocaine, eh.

KITTY: That ain't one snowball to the sex blizzard I been giving.

(Beat)

KANAKA: Eh, Kitty. How come you no do da kine with me, eh? I been thinking. You do it with haoles, Flips, Pakes, Portagis, Buddhaheads, even Samoans. Everybody. Except Hawaiian. Eh? That's how come you no do it with me. Not because of my diseases. Not because of my smell. It's something else, ain't it, Kitty. It's because of my blood. *(Beat)* Maybe you look at me and see you. Like look in one mirror. You see your eyes in mine. What, if you do it with me, you think it be like doing it to yourself? *(Beat)* Look what they do to you every night. *(Beat)* You diseased, too. C'mon, Princess, that's how come, eh. You Hawaiian like me.

(JAMES enters. KIMO has become JAMES. He wears long pants, shiny shoes, and a long-sleeved shirt that is crisp and buttoned at the top. He carries a full sack of religious items and a Bible.)

JAMES: *(Simply)* Kanak, get out my bar.

(KANAKA turns, sees JAMES, and bursts out laughing.)

KANAKA: That's funny, Kimo. Some kinda costume? You think it Halloween, dress-up like one haole? Or you do da kine stand-up comedy?

JAMES: My name James.

KANAKA: James?

KITTY: Your name Kimo.

KANAKA: Oh, you little haole boy? You go eat potato now instead of rice?

(JAMES *hangs a large steel crucifix on the wall. He takes various religious articles out of his sack and places them around the bar. He has statues, vigil lights, scapulars, etc. He takes down various "heathen" adornments such as half-naked Hawaiian dancers and Tiki statues. He begins to convert the bar into a shrine.*)

KITTY: What you doing to the bar?

KANAKA: No matter how flipped out you are, Flip, you still owe us money. Pay day for us, but pay-up day for you.

JAMES: How come I owe?

KANAKA: You no pay, I broke your leg, that's how come.

(JAMES *puts a piece of paper on the bar.*)

JAMES: Pay-up day for you. This your bill.

(KANAKA *rips it up.*)

KANAKA: What bill? (*He laughs grotesquely.*)

JAMES: (*Writing another bill quickly*) This bill. One-hundred forty-five dollars and thirty-three cents. Tax included.

KANAKA: You been smokin' or what, brah? Gimme one beer.

JAMES: No more free drinks for nobody.

KITTY: That's it, Kimo. You tell him. It's about time this pig start paying. Thing's gonna be different around here, you piece of bacon.

JAMES: No pay, no drinks.

KITTY: Tell it like it is, brah.

JAMES: No rent, no room.

KITTY: What?

KANAKA: Huh?

JAMES: You gotta move outta the back room. No more prostitutes in my bar.

(Beat)

KANAKA: One more time, brah.

KITTY: No act, Kimo.

JAMES: Not. I no like stay ugly no more. I like one pretty place. Good people. Happy, safe life. Nice things for once. Clean dreams.

KITTY: You make me feel dirty.

JAMES: Maybe you gotta feel dirty so you can wash and come clean.

KITTY: You like rent, I pay rent.

JAMES: Too late. I like you out.

KITTY: We been together for so long. Seem like all our life. I can't remember not knowing you.

JAMES: And all that time you use me. Like one bar rag. No more.

KITTY: This not you talking. Those not your eyes. Tell me you no mean this. No do this. Stop when you still can, Kimo. Run from that Hunter. Run free.

(Beat)

JAMES: Free like you? *(Beat)* You one whore. *(Beat)* I look at you and I like for throw-up.

(Silence)

KITTY: *(Deeply hurt)* When you like me out?

JAMES: Tomorrow. I like start my new life now.

KITTY: That's what you like, that's what you get.

KANAKA: *(Burning)* Eh, manong, you cracked or what? You no talk to Kitty like that. You in big trouble, pally. She Yakuza. Omuro no gonna like this. You better think twice or go buy some crutches. Last time, Flip. Keep Kitty! Gimme beer! Gimme money!

JAMES: Go rot in hell.

KITTY: Kimo!

KANAKA: Okay, cripple. You no pay-up, you get bust up.

(KANAKA grabs JAMES violently.)

KITTY: Leave him alone!

KANAKA: I hate for do this to you, you mop up for me, but this gonna hurt.

(KITTY jumps on KANAKA's back. REV enters through the front door with his revolver drawn.)

REV: Freeze.

KANAKA: Get outta here, shark. This my job.

REV: This my job, too. James is C C. Let him go.

KANAKA: What?

KITTY: Hunter wen convert Kimo!

KANAKA: No wonder he acting lolo.

REV: I'm here for you, Pigface. Taking you in for the tourist murder.

KANAKA: I never murder nobody. I never even seen the guy.

REV: Oh, yeah? You look like pals in this picture. *(He holds up a photograph.)* Snapped right before you butchered him in cold blood.

KANAKA: Kimo! I kill you! You turn into one canary for the C C? You convert from coolie to stoolie!

REV: *(Strongly)* Let him go or I shoot.

(KANAKA *releases* JAMES.)

JAMES: I wen give him the picture of you and the tourist for your own good. And I gonna testify in court against you for save your soul.

REV: Let's go. You've got a date with an iron cage.

KANAKA: Uh-uh. Wait one minute. Something the matter here. Yeah, I know. The C C protects murderers from the law.

REV: Only through confession.

KANAKA: Whatever that is, I do it!

REV: No dice.

KANAKA: Eh, you wen baptize me, brah. I C C. You gotta confess me!

(Beat)

REV: Guess you've caught me on a technicality. *(Beat)* Pay James or no absolution. *(To* KIMO*)* Add a bottle of white wine to his bill.

KANAKA: Eh!

(KANAKA *pays* JAMES. JAMES *puts a bottle of white wine on the bar.*)

REV: Keep your accounts clean, Kanaka, in heaven and on Earth. Two glasses, please, James.

(JAMES *places the glasses next to the wine.*)

KANAKA: *(Suddenly terrified)* You ain't gonna change me, yeah? No do me like you wen did Kimo. Lock me up if you gonna try make me not me.

REV: Mind if we use your bar, James?

JAMES: I go out front, keep customers out.

REV: All churches should be bars. Attendance would go up.

KITTY: Send mine 'round the back, eh?

JAMES: I no do that no more.

KITTY: I forget. Habit, I guess. I gotta go pack anyway.

(JAMES *exits out the front door.*)

KITTY: Dig one hole and watch them fight for jump in. I like kill you for convert Kimo. You wait, haole. The lava gonna fly.

(KITTY *exits into the backroom.* REV *holsters his revolver and takes the wine and glasses to a table. He sits.*)

REV: Sit.

(KANAKA *sits at the table.* REV *takes out a small pouch and removes a communion host.*)

REV: This is my body. Eat me.

(Pause)

KANAKA: You make me puke.

REV: *(Breaking the host in two)* Eat it.

(KANAKA *eats half,* REV *the other.* REV *pours wine into the glasses.*)

REV: This is my blood. Drink it.

KANAKA: I not one vampire.

(They both drink.)

REV: Give me some money.

(KANAKA *gives him a couple of dollars.*)

REV: I've gotta say Mass. That's how I collect.

KANAKA: More better for bust bones.

REV: *(Placing a stole around his neck)* Relax. It's really wine. Who's killing the sugar men?

KANAKA: What's that gotta do with the tourist?

REV: I'm running this confession! You want protection or a steel box?

(Beat)

KANAKA: Unifac owns the sugar companies. The companies go broke. So Unifac's gotta sell them. Yakuza like for buy. But Unifac, they no like for sell to the Japanese crime, yeah. So the Yakuza knock off Unifac's top men one by one until they sell them to the Yakuza. Simple. No big deal.

REV: Why does the Yakuza want the cane fields?

KANAKA: They no tell me that stuff. I jus' crack necks.

REV: You didn't kill those sugar men. They were executed clean. One bullet through the brain. You're messy. They murder with the mind. You kill with your heart.

KANAKA: I gotta believe in what I do.

REV: One question. The tourist's body was punctured with what looked like boar tusks.

KANAKA: You like that one, eh? Well, me, I figure I fool everybody, yeah. I put the dead body inside the bag, then throw the haole into the back of my pick-up truck. I drive to the garbage dump. I could get rid of him inside the compacter, but no, I get more better idea. I wait in the dark for the wild boar for come. I know she come to the dump at night. And then I hear one. Bugger come real slow, yeah. Sniff out for humans. She no smell me. Bugger come near. I make my move. The pig scared, squeal, run. I jump on her back. Pull out my knife. Cut her neck. Ooh, the bugger let out one big wet groan. I grab the tusk. Pull the neck back. Snap. Limp. Makee. *(Beat)* The moon bright. I cut out one tusk. Take the body out from the bag. In the moonlight, I stick the tusk into the pukas the knife we make in the haole. I go back to Kilauea. Shove him down the throat of the volcano. Feed him to the crater. The haole like it here so bad, he can stay for good. This not his island.

REV: But the body was naked. If you wanted to fool everyone and make it look like the guy was attacked by a wild boar, he would have had some clothes on.

(Beat)

KANAKA: Oh, yeah. *(Beat)* Eh, sometimes I think I more better go up Mauna Loa. Live on berries and game. When I go up the mountain all my allergies stop. My skin come clean. The air different. Me, I allergic to everything. Alcohol. Cigarettes. Haoles. Before the haoles come, there was no disease. Not even the common cold. Can you think of that? But the haoles come bring their white death. Now everything infection. I think more better, me, I live before the haoles. My ancestors was royalty, you know. Now everything die. Not that many full-blooded Hawaiians left. One doctor tell me, eh, I allergic to myself. But not when I go mauka, up the mountain. When I come to town, that's when I like get everything I no can have. Like Kitty.

REV: Why do you want Kitty?

KANAKA: 'Cause I no can have her. *(Beat)* I never can get no woman. Not even one prostitute. Nobody like touch me. Nobody. Sometimes me, I get this feeling deep inside of me and I jus' like for explode. Like one volcano. Like last night. My skin crawl then I bust out. I think maybe if somebody jus' touch me once in a while, I'd be all right. You know? When I go touch Kitty, she yells and moves away. But when I hit her, she stay still. She no let me hug her, but she let me hit her. So I hit her for touch her. She no like me hit her in the face, so I try not to. But if somebody jus' let me touch them, eh, I no try hit Kitty. Maybe. *(Beat)* I get this one dream about Kitty, always stay the same. Over and over again. I know what's gonna happen. It's Kitty. She walks up to me real slow. Then puts one

finger on my lip, and rubs, back and forth. So soft. Like
nobody I ever know. Then last night. In real life. She
wen touch me. No kidding. Jus' like that. In this bar. I
thought dreams was just dreams. You know, the thing
that never comes true. But last night, my dream come
true. Kitty wen walk up and touch my lip like that. Jus'
like my dreams.

REV: You don't want to sleep with Kitty.

KANAKA: Yes, I do.

REV: I don't think so.

KANAKA: I'm a man. She's everything I like.

REV: I think you just want her to look at you. Like you.
Touch your lip once in a while.

KANAKA: I like her for look into my eyes and see me.

REV: You want her to dream of you, like you dream of
her.

KANAKA: I like her for dream of me.

REV: You're not the same as everyone. You're different.
You want to be different to her. You want to be special,
like she's special to you. Kitty's not just anyone.

KANAKA: She's special to me.

REV: She's not just a woman. She's Kitty. Not no one.
Someone. Different. Like you. You're different.

KANAKA: Me, I different. I not the same.

REV: Everyone sleeps with Kitty. It's different not to
sleep with her. Only certain special people don't sleep
with Kitty. Like Kimo.

KANAKA: Kimo and her stay close.

REV: Kimo doesn't sleep with her. You want to be close
to her. You don't want to sleep with her.

KANAKA: Yeah, I different, eh. 'Cause me, I no like sleep with her. 'Cause then I special to her.

REV: The unique doesn't sleep with her, only the common do.

KANAKA: See, me, I feel close to her. She's special to me. I love her. What? What I wen said? I love her. I no like sleep with her, I jus' like for love her. Protect her. Like Kimo. But Kimo not Kimo no more. I try be like Kimo. And I can really protect her. You'll see. And we'll be special for each other. I no go hit her and then maybe she go touch my lip. I love her.

REV: Was Omuro in on this alone?

KANAKA: Him and some fat cat from the mainland. *(Beat)* Eh, what I wen said? I mixed up with this love stuff.

REV: What does Kanaka mean in Hawaiian?

KANAKA: Human being.

REV: For the record, did you kill the tourist?

KANAKA: Yeah.

REV: *(Blessing him)* I forgive you in nomine Patris, et Filii, et Spiritus Sancti. I bury your sins within my heart. Go in peace and sin no more. That means don't kill any more tourists.

KANAKA: Okay. I protected or what?

REV: Yeah.

KANAKA: All right. Eh, Father, thanks for straightening me out about Kitty.

REV: Comes with the collar.

(KANAKA *runs to the backroom and pounds on the door.)*

KANAKA: Hey, Kitty! We 'ohana now. Special.

(KITTY *enters, wearing a lava-lava and a print top.)*

KITTY: What's the matter, you stupid or what?

KANAKA: I finally figured it out. Everything good. I no hit you no more. I protect you. I go do anything you say.

KITTY: *(To* REV*)* You wen did him, too, eh.

REV: And he told me all about you and that fat cat from the mainland.

KITTY: *(To* KANAKA*)* Pupule! *(To* REV*)* So what, I wen did that guy Red one time. What you gonna do, call the cops?

(A storm breaks. Lightening scratches across the bar through the picture window. Rain falls. Thunder. JAMES *is pushed into the bar.* OMURO *enters. He is Japanese, dressed in a three-piece suit with silk tie and handkerchief, and carries a submachine gun.)*

OMURO: His piece.

*(*KANAKA *takes* REV's *revolver and points it at* REV.*)*

OMURO: I warn you once with that note. Patience running out.

REV: Didn't catch the name, pal.

KANAKA: This Omuro.

OMURO: *(Raising the gun)* Hear my confession.

REV: When an operative's in a jam, he hears confession. Spill it.

OMURO: What you think this all about? Drugs. What else? Japan call it the white death. Here call it cocaine. Cane fields front for drug trade. Dope in the sugar shipments. Sugar can go everywhere, baby. Make the whole world sweet. Locals keep job cut cane. We build the Buddhist temples. Everybody get fat, happy, and Buddhist. Forgive me, Father, for I am going to sin. *(He cocks the machine gun.)*

REV: *(Blessing* OMURO, *deadpan)* I absolve you in the name of the Father, and of the Son, and of the Holy Spirit.

OMURO: Amen. Now that you forgive me, you are harmless. You cannot tell one soul. The C C most wonderful corporation. Go home, Hunter, there no more game for you here. *(Taking out a large bag of cocaine)* Here kitty, kitty, kitty.

*(*KITTY *offers* OMURO *her open mouth. He licks his finger, dips it into the cocaine, and rubs it onto her gums.)*

OMURO: Nice kitty. You go to Buddha study?

KITTY: Once a week.

OMURO: Kanaka?

KANAKA: Me, too.

OMURO: Excellent. Only Buddha can save you, baby. *(Looking out the picture window)* Ah! And the Buddha getting ready erupt his crater. Maybe I turn this bar into temple in honor Buddha's volcanic power. Statue Buddha look excellent where that crucifix hangs. This his island, now. And the Buddha is happy.

KITTY: Pele still live here.

OMURO: Nobody convert to Pele. She washed up. Jesus, too. But Buddha doing excellent.

KITTY: I no like the cut you take on my personal clients.

OMURO: Standard for Yashiwara. All Tokyo, Honolulu chicks.

KITTY: My clients stay mine. That was the deal.

OMURO: Deals change, baby.

KITTY: Not with me. This not your body.

OMURO: *(Erupting)* When I tell Kimo pay, he pay, Kanaka collect, he collect, Hunter forgive, he forgive. When I tell you trick, you trick.

KITTY: Buddha no sit on this crater. Pele gon blow your Buddha back to Japan. Shoot the hot lava under his fat okole.

(KITTY *dumps the bag of cocaine onto* OMURO's *head. He knocks the bag away, spins his machine gun around to everyone, then aims at* KANAKA. KANAKA *is pointing* REV's *revolver at* OMURO. *Silence*)

OMURO: Put down gun, Kanaka.

KANAKA: No. *(Beat)* Bust your own bones. This not your island.

OMURO: Tsk, tsk, tsk. You better hide deep in the hapu'u, pig. You sign your own contract, baby. *(To* KITTY*)* And you, pussy-cat, you work nowhere. Not Honolulu, San Fran, L A, D C. Not all Kittys have nine lives. *(To* REV*)* Hunter. You're so cool. Don't you ever see Red? *(Smiling)* Shaka, brahs.

(OMURO *backs out the door, still aiming the machine gun at* KANAKA, *and exits. When the door is opened, the wind whistles, rain falls, thunder.* REV *goes to the phone booth and dials. It rings until* CODE *picks up.*)

KANAKA: That Buddhahead mean business. And the crater. Come with me, Kitty. I protect you. We go mauna, hele, up the mountain.

KITTY: With you? You lolo? I no need run from the crater. Pele no gonna hurt me. She protect me, not you, hog. This my last night in the Volcano Bar. I stay right here. You say you go do what I say, Kanak? Well, I say split.

KANAKA: If that's what you like. *(He exits through the backroom, still carrying* REV's *revolver.)*

KITTY: Eh, not through my room! *(To* JAMES*)* I forget. Not my room no more. *(She sits and takes cocaine.)*

CODE: *(A voice over the phone)* The Cardinal Code.

REV: *(Into phone)* Hey. Red.

CODE: Yes?

REV: Hunter.

CODE: *(Laughing)* No one has called me Red since—

REV: Your last trip to Honolulu. Stiffs are piling up down here. The heat's up.

CODE: Then I'll pull you out right now. Three murders in three days is a burn.

(Beat)

REV: What three murders? *(Beat)* Wrong response, Code. *(Beat)* I never told you about Lionel Harding. Or the tourist. *(Beat)* Did I? *(Beat)* But then I didn't have to. *(Beat)* Just had a little chat with your buddy. Old Buddha-breath. Force-confession from a Buddhist? Jeez, that's no inside job, huh? You write that cute little note or did Omuro come up with that himself? I don't like threats on my life. Especially from my boss.

CODE: I don't know what you're talking about.

REV: Maybe Rome does. Life everlasting—

CODE: Wait. Calm down. *(Beat)* All right. *(Beat)* The Chicago Chancery owns the sugar land. *(Beat)* We lease to Unifac. They went bankrupt; now we'll lease to the Yakuza. They'll do well; we get a cut. Progress is made by compromise, Rev. Like all corporations, self-preservation is first. Then, we can do good. You know that. We'll feed and clothe the poor with this money. We can't stop human nature, but we can utilize conversion. Clean dirty money. Convert bad into good. *(Beat)* Rome sent you to investigate because they want the deal for themselves. *(Beat)* Stick with us. You're still an American. I'll make it worth your while. *(Beat)* How did you know it was me?

REV: I didn't. *(Beat)* About my assignment. How do you convert the C C? *(He rips the phone out of the booth. Thunder booms.)*

JAMES: You all right, Reverend? *(Beat)* We gotta go. The eruption.

REV: I'm not going anywhere, Kimo.

JAMES: My name James.

REV: You're as Hebrew as pork.

JAMES: You wen baptize me.

REV: To get information. *(Beat)* The game's up. The whole thing's a bust. *(Beat)* Listen. You went for the restaurant, pal. Don't come off thinking it was something else.

JAMES: But—

REV: Get outta here. Beat it. Before I deconvert you. Yeah. Maybe that's what I should do. Go back across the world and deconvert my converts. *(He takes a big drink from a Jack Daniels bottle.)*

JAMES: You turning on the C C?

REV: Maybe I've always been a double-agent and never knew it. You hear me? Get outta here.

JAMES: You tell me get out my own bar? *(Beat)* This all been one act? You wen lied to me this whole time?

(Beat)

REV: Yeah.

(Beat)

KITTY: When you grow up, you wanna be jus' like Rev Hunter, yeah, Kimo?

(Pause)

JAMES: You both go to hell. *(He exits.)*

KITTY: Kimo!

(REV *slams the bar.*)

KITTY: You one messed-up haole bugger.

REV: An accomplice to my own murder case. Sent here to find who? Myself? Hunter hunts Hunter. But what do I convert myself into?

KITTY: How come you gotta convert people, anyhow? I no like other people for believe in Pele. She my goddess. But you, you hold a gun to other people's temples.

(REV *takes a drink from the bottle, then pours into a glass with no ice.*)

REV: I think I just excommunicated myself. So it's all history. Wanna drink?

KITTY: I stick with this. (*She snorts a line of cocaine.*) I wen quit, too. No more Yakuza for me. I never get one pimp; I no need no corporate pimp, now. I stand by myself. Again. No more organization.

REV: That's me. Un-organized.

(*She does another line of cocaine.*)

KITTY: Y'know, think about it. Me and you, we get the two oldest con-jobs in the world. (*Beat*) Only one thing different. I give them what they pay for.

(*Kilauea erupts. There is a deep explosion. The Volcano Bar shakes. Bottles rattle. The bar reflects the scarlet motion of the shooting lava. A red glow shows through the cracks in the floorboards. They watch the eruption through the picture window and are bathed in red light.*)

KITTY: The eruption. (*Beat*) We stay above the flow; we're safe.

REV: (*Watching the eruption*) So that's how this island is made. Burning it down and building it up. And men killing each other over it. For their gods. (*Beat*) What if a volcano was just a volcano? Wouldn't it all be a sin?

(KANAKA *enters, carrying* REV's *revolver and covered with snow. The crater continues to erupt.*)

KANAKA: The sky bust open! Snow blizzard. Ice cubes. But the crater still erupt. The volcano crazy. Come with me, Kitty.

KITTY: We're safe now.

REV: I'm sorry for everything I did to you, Kanaka.

KANAKA: You no did nothing to me. Come, Kitty.

KITTY: Not. I'm okay here.

REV: *(Suddenly antagonistic)* Yeah. That's right. She's with me. Mine.

(REV *grabs* KITTY.)

KANAKA: What you doing?

REV: I take what I want from here. Like everybody else. And I'm taking her. What are you gonna do about it?

(REV *twists* KITTY's *arm behind her back.*)

KITTY: Oww. What's the matter with you?

KANAKA: No do that.

REV: Why not? You're not going to stop me. You don't have the guts anymore.

KITTY: Let go.

KANAKA: *(Raising* REV's *revolver)* Stop.

REV: You're not gonna pull the trigger. You're gonna let me yank the tusks right outta your mouth. Aren't you, Pigface.

KANAKA: Let her go.

REV: What are you waiting for? Or did I do you like you did the tourist? Huh? Do it. I dare you.

(REV *pushes* KITTY *away and shoves his forehead right to the barrel of the revolver in* KANAKA's *hand.*)

REV: Do it. Do it!

(KANAKA *pulls the trigger. The revolver clicks rapidly, slows down, and then stops.*)

REV: That's the old Kanaka I know. *(Beat)* My gun's never been loaded.

(Beat)

KITTY: What?

REV: Fifth Commandment. I play by the Book. I don't kill anyone. No matter how much good it does.

KANAKA: You wen baptize me with no bullets?

(Beat)

REV: *(To* KITTY*)* Sorry about getting rough with you.

KITTY: I can handle one collar.

KANAKA: I wen stand up to Omuro with a toy gun?

REV: It's all a bluff. All of it. A big, big bluff.

(*A man in a hooded raincoat bursts in through the backroom.* REV *turns toward him. The man raises a gun and fires.* REV *and* KITTY *fall to the floor.* KANAKA *runs, opens the front door, and just as he's about to exit—*)

MAN: Stop!

(KANAKA *freezes.*)

MAN: Turn around. Hele!

(KANAKA *faces him. The man drops his hood. He is* JAMES.)

JAMES: Kanak. Leave. My. Bar.

KANAKA: Whatever you say, Boss.

(JAMES *smiles and raises his gun.* KANAKA *jumps through the front door as* JAMES *opens fire.* JAMES *runs to the door and fires into the darkness, snow, and wind. He closes the door, then takes off his raincoat. He is dressed in an elegant tuxedo. He lights a cigarette which is at the end of a long*

cigarette holder, and takes a puff. He goes to the bar phone,
takes out the card, and dials. It rings.)

CODE: *(A voice over the phone)* The Cardinal Code.

JAMES: *(Into the phone)* James.

CODE: Is it done?

JAMES: Yes.

CODE: Deconversion can't be tolerated. He knew that.
Your namesake was an apostle, James. A fisherman.
Would you like to be a fisher of men?

JAMES: I do what you say, your Eminence. *(Beat)* I wen
did Kitty. Omuro say.

CODE: She was a good girl. I absolve you in nomine
Patris, et Filii, et Spiritus Sancti. I hold your sins
within my heart. Go back to Omuro. He'll take care of
everything. You'll get your restaurant. Life everlasting.

JAMES: Amen. *(He hangs up the phone. Standing over*
REV:*)* It's. My. Bar. *(Beat)* Mine. *(He goes to* KITTY.*)* I'm
sorry, Kitty. *(Beat)* But I'm forgiven. *(He backs away.)*
I'm forgiven.

*(*JAMES *exits through the front door.* KANAKA *immediately*
enters through the back room. He kneels beside KITTY *and*
props her dead body against himself.)

KANAKA: Look, Kitty. The volcano no cry for you. It
jus' lava. *(Beat)* I go up the mountain now. No Buddha.
No Jesus. No Pele. Jus' the crater. I take you with me.
(He picks her up.) Sleep, Princess. You safe, now.

*(*KANAKA *exits with* KITTY'*s body through the front door.*
REV *sits up. Then stands. He takes off his jacket, then his*
clerical collar and vest. He touches where the bullets hit the
bullet-proof vest. He looks out the picture window.)

REV: First thing you learn in the seminary is how to
play dead. *(He discards the collar and vest. He wears a*
black tee shirt. He watches the eruption through the picture

window as crimson washes over him.) Best view on the island.

*(*REV *finishes the Jack Daniels in his glass and exits through the backroom as the blood-red lights slowly fade. Blackout.)*

END OF PLAY